From the Margins

Nathan Moore

PandaMonk
PUBLISHING

ISBN-13: 978-0990517665

ISBN-10: 0990517667

PandaMonk Publishing, LLC

Alexandria, Virginia

Table of Contents

FROM THE MARGINS

Find a Girl to Love

I remember the rain came
it came from up above

I was there when the sun came down
and said find someone to love

You've got to find a girl to love

Generation Kill

The closest I've been to war
is what I see on TV

Generation kill
yeah that's just not for me

I don't know what you do
but I do things

They're turning all my friends
into killing machines

But they won't get me

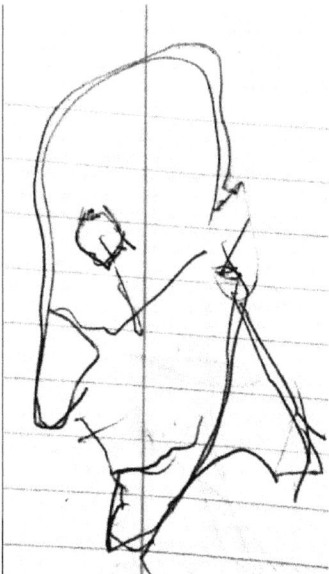

Love is Strange

Love is strange
love is a stranger to me

Play the game
and you will see

I drink so much
I should be a fish in the sea

I used to be King
King of the Thieves
when I worked at Macys

But out here
we float all day
the only thing worth stealing
is a million miles away

We're just two lost souls
swimming in an Earth-sized
fish bowl
light year after light year

But now it's 3010
and here we are again

fishing off the same damn pier

waiting for the queen

That Other Place

I want a lover I don't have to love

so we can float above

all that's killing us

all that's killing me

is stuck on repeat

I see it on TV

I run into it on the street

and it's telling me

to obey my feet

to cut off my wings

to care about Earthly things

forget about that girl that made you sing

here's one that can make you think

no wait, better yet

here's one that can't do a thing

she just sits and waits

for that fateful day

when the world turns over

and it's off to that other place

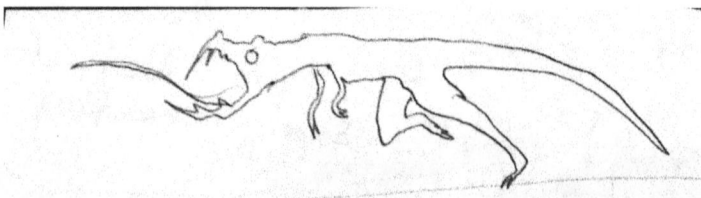

Playing God

Hanging out
in a crowd
that's full of thieves
and
stupid dreamers

No
you'd never understand

All I
want to do
is lay around
and waste some time
with you

We'll sleep outside
beneath the stars
while everyone else
is playing god

Making money
don't seem so hard
we can drive around
in fancy cars

We can stay out late
at all the bars
we can order drinks
on credit cards
now if I only had a job

Yeah, I'll take the money
and run
no, you won't find me

Yeah, I'll just take the money
and run

Things ain't
how they used to be
when everything
was in front of me

Now it's all gone
and I'm still here
and all that's left
is the fear
that there's no god

No, there's no god

I Need You to Know This

I'm in the sun
looking away from you

I gave a second to the breeze

I am the one
who is taking the absolute

The way I'm bending like a tree

But you can take from me
you can always take from me

I'll never ask of you
not you

I'm getting tired of the evening view
I'll settle for a morning with no sun
but only if it's with you

So what if I confess
to stealing your last cigarette

You say you're not impressed
I need you to know this

I'm standing on the edge
I'm looking down and it's permanent

There's no saving grace from them
yeah they need me to know this

They need me to know

Casper the Fucking Ghost

When loving me gets hard
I'll understand where you're
coming from

When meeting face to face
is even out of place
my god...

Waking up is hard
it's all I was living for

I'm the walking dead
and I'm knocking at your door

Let me in
I'm not a ghost
I don't want your soul

I'm walking through walls
while you're getting calls
from boys who have a pulse

So bestill my beating heart
or let me go

Stick Up

I've been around so many towns
they all seem the same

I've seen the fall of many men
but they never complain

I've seen the ones
the ones with guns
they say they're gonna
rob this place

I say I don't know the way
but they shoot me down any way

Ghost World

When I was young
I was free

When I used to run
there was so much more air
to breathe

But now I'm a stranger
instead of a loner
in this wicked little town
that looks like a ghost world

I was where the ghosts were

They sent me over
to get a closer view

When I Woke Up

It's been a long
quiet
drive

There's a hotel on the corner
a rest stop at the border

This road goes for miles

I never found
Love
in Virginia

I've searched
from here
to California

I've flown on a plane
to Chicago

I only stayed
a few days
but it seemed longer

I took some pills
to help me sleep

When I woke up…

Fish Boy

I fell into a pond
when I was eight years old

But then a hand
tore through the moss
and pulled me above

But now it's getting harder
to breathe
with these slits in my throat
I want to scream
at the sight of a boat
I want to eat
things that live in the ground
I hide under my bed
when the birds come around

My parents thought I should learn to swim
the day I turned ten
but to their surprise I was good
shit, I was great!
I did ten fucking laps
around the whole god damn lake

But now I'm feeling strange
with these scales on my face
I want to curl up and die
when a girl walks my way
because she doesn't see
a boy who she'd want to date
just a freak
standing in her way
I want to scream
throw my fins in the air
is there someone
somewhere…

I'm going home
beneath the green uncertainty
I want to watch the world from afar
that's just not a part of me

That day I changed
in those few seconds underwater
I saw every part of god's Earth
and it was beautiful

Are You Cold When Made a Drifter?

We sat behind the wind beaten trees of West Virginia
and talked of secret limbs that would never splinter

The cheap wine and vodka
carried the blood from our toes to our faces

And somewhere in the night
we filled up all of our empty spaces

Young Love

I was sharpening my pencil
looking at your paper
looking dumb

I was scared

I was young

You held my hand in the hall
I felt weird and tall

Two weeks later I felt it all
Love and Pain and Hurt

You asked me to come out
I was tired and you were loud

So you went away in a room
he laid you down
and kissed your head

You let him undress you
and lay next to you
while I was in bed sleeping softly

I'm not ready

Let me sleep until morning

I Am

I am through with tedious
impressions

I am blank
paint me gray

There's no call
no calm that's
missing

Most of all
I'm unimpressed

Erasing all that gives me
clearance
to parade again

I adhere to the
distant

The call
the calm
the next

Sarah Tonin

Some days
I feel like getting high
any way

Sarah told me to stay

Sarah told me to play

Some days
I smoke cigarettes
just to stay awake

And when there's pain
I take blue pills so I can feel again

Sarah

No One Knows the Back Roads

You're not alone
but you're lonely

You get out of bed
but you're not ready

It's twenty five for an eighth today
that won't break my piggy bank

No one knows the back roads like we do

My friend left to fight a war today
yeah, we'll have the tequila ready
when he gets back to the states

Is he scared
of dying?

He'd say
"Hell no!"

Time Spent in Parking Lots

I look up from the steering wheel
mouth dry
muscles stiffening
an un-inspirational sky
looming over the endless rows
of office buildings

It's 9:15 a.m.

I won't be myself for the next 8 hours
I'm sick now
the possibility of my facade collapsing mid-day
doesn't sound as farfetched as I want it to

I strain to produce saliva in my mouth
so at least I'm able to talk
my lips crack open
and the stinging in the back of my throat is pushed
forward

Waking every limb in my body
I start for the door

Suite 102
Office Building 420

It seems miles away

but here

there is no middle ground

I'm halfway there and there's no turning back

I close my eyes and the concrete walls swallow me

I look up from the steering wheel and strain to listen

for the low rumble of a world ending tidal wave

but I'm consumed with the humming of my car engine

droning on

blocking out every subtle nuance

that a slight shift within our tectonic plates could create

I want the ground to open up

and swallow this single parking space

nothing else

One more hour until my day will begin

or nine more until it ends?

The days seem to just blend into each other

faster than usual

Wake up

work

sleep

What day is it?

It's 9:15 once again and this little parking lot is empty
not a single tire has touched this pavement except for mine

Every morning I pull into this same parking space
and turn off my engine

This hunk of rock is here to greet me
with gray indifference

Yet the time spent here is the best time of the day

Time spent in parking lots

Down

She took me down to
the end
of my street

We kissed like children do
when they're scared
and inexperienced

And then her hands went
down
down

Down

The Blues

I'd play you a song
but I
sold my guitar

I needed the money
but that didn't get me
real far

I'd sing of my love for you
night and day

But all of my friends
they tell me that
I can't sing

Maybe it's true
but all I have to say is

FU-

UCK-

YOU!

I'd give you everything
but I'm so

So

So

Broke

I'd even steal for you
if everybody around here
didn't already know
I was a crook

Yeah, everybody around here
already knows
that I'm a crook

Oh baby please
you got me down on my knees

I don't know what to think

I got nowhere to go
no one to see
nothing to smoke
nothing to drink

And now I'm without you

Sand

I found my girl
under the killing moon
she'll probably kill me soon
but god!
I love the way she moves!

I go down to the drug store stand
to see the drug store man
because he's always got
the *good* news

I look around and all I see is sand
all I see is sand
and it's coming for me
and you

Strawberry Vodka for Napoleon

I've had many
many jobs

Most just to meet
an end

End of the day
Week
Month
Year

The Sun comes back
to greet me
and says
"Holy shit,
he's still here!"

Yes I'm still here
but there's beauty in it
somewhere

I haven't seen the forests
the mountains
the oceans
but the back of the work stations

Stock rooms
Offices
Kitchens

Don't get me started on
the Kitchens

I hate these jobs
for so many reasons
and I love them
for only one

I love where they led me
on those rainy work days

Pass out these flyers
Ok!

Throw them away

Greet the day
find the places
where we can sit and get paid

Just to sit?

I need some distraction
so I went to the library

sometimes drunk off of
Passion

There during the hours
I was on the clock
I began reading
shelf after
shelf

On the Road
led to
Stranger places

Hemingway and
Crime
and Punishment
captured me secretly

I wanted to bash that old lady's
head in too

To be a Napoleon
just for a moment

I brought books to bars
and started smoking and
reading

A hard habit to quit

A woman once said
"Who reads a book in
a bar?"

Her lovely drunk posture
led her onto my shoulder
and she glimpsed a page of
The Portrait of the Artist
as a Young Man

Little did she know
that I had just been scared
to death
of hell

I could feel the flames

Religion didn't have shit
on James

She took another shot

I turned the page

Once I worked at night
where we would scurry out

from behind

the walls

like insects in the dark

and put little boxes on

shelves

and push carts

Free Bird

on repeat

Beetle backed

managers

making calculations for

next week

Here I heard talk of a

Man

who was a

Drunk

a dirty

Drunk

He worked many jobs

He wrote many lines

I followed the scent of the
Ink
and found poetry
in his hung over rants

Sorry Robert Frost
…Style…

I'm with you on the telescopes though
in every town…

Every town
but mine

The drunken poet prevails
his words were exactly
what I needed
explained this place
these faces
perfectly

I can feel the social
organism
Breathe
Wheeze
Cough
Choke

Work harder
help it become strong

Or find the Foundation
somewhere near the end
of Space

Only to land on
a desert world

Sand and
no rain

I've had the job
of being a student

Thank you Holden

I've had the job
of being a salesman

A soulless vessel
doomed to crash
and burn
and in that wreckage
find Men in High Castles
and men here on Earth

who died but still
grasp us

Century old words
sent to the future
to warn

To welcome
whatever comes

And it came
only I missed it

I was collecting sawdust
off a concrete floor
and missed it like
the shooting star
that to me
never happened

For you
it was beautiful

Once in a life time

I'm tired already
but my hands don't show it

It's in my head

slowing me down

to drunk speeds

I still work these jobs

Delivery Driver

Hand for Hire

Drug Buyer

and small time

Supplier

Liar

Breaker of

Entrances

Tear the gate

off the hinges

Pry open windows

with tools

Stolen

Expensive

Photographer

Dishwasher

Take a picture of

This

This running around
Tired
Excluded
from the real life
that men
once pursued

But they all died
I'll die too

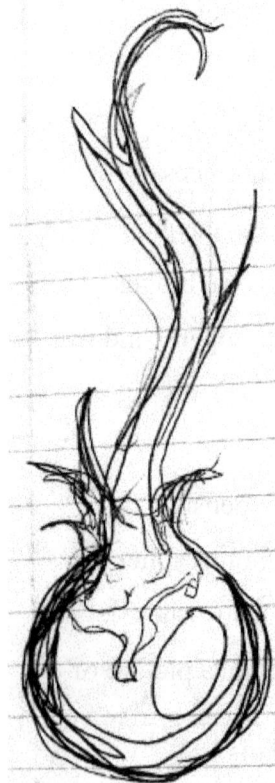

I Found You That Day in a Field of Wires

I look around and can't help but
hate
what we've done to the place

I'm walking beside this retired
warship
searching for shade

All I see is metal
and steel
some trees for
decoration

Jellyfish bob
up
and
down
in the water

Behind the buildings
there are
Chinese fish
you can feed bread
and quarters

Here are the kind
of people that
run
do laps around the pier

I've never known
one of these
sweat drenched
maniacs
running in rain
or snow
or heat

Today the weather
compliments
the beautiful parts
the rest is out of place

Noise
Cars

And the silent warship
with tourists aboard

I take another look
around

nothing good yet
nothing new

Just more construction
pushing us away
from
the cities

Trying to find
solace
in the remaining
parks
and
lakes

Now we're forced to
get away
take trips to
the real
places

The forest
the ocean

They charge admission
for shade these
days

Nothing to do except
return to my own car
my own city
construction
torn up roads

Leading to
nowhere

I've been driving for hours
now
trying to get reception
trying to connect with you
on this lonely
afternoon

I finally found
you
in a field of wires

Under the satellites
and towers
bringing us together

In those moments
all the warships sink
in the harbor

On those days I look

around

and see you

in everything

Brake Lights

The final overpass
flew over my head

We hit the traffic and
stood
still

A few buildings
had lights strung out
across the window sills
or multi-colored
Christmas trees
floating on wires

All I could see now
were car brake lights
blurred and dragged
across the sky

My eyes were squinting
I had been crying

I opened up the
passenger side door

and stepped
out into the road

I told my sister
and Richie
to find me
later
or I would
find
them

I walk in between
the cars
spewing smoke

Drivers hang
outside of their windows
yelling and screaming

On the sidewalk
I follow
a group of people
that looked
like they knew
where

they were
going

A police man waved us on
Cross!

We huddled together
and moved faster
partly because
of the cop
partly because
it was just so
damn
cold

Up ahead I could see
the road
blocked off

There were hundreds of people
on each side
of the street
watching giant balloons
and bands
pass by

I followed an
inflated star
to a bench
where I sat
and watched
its body
block out the moon

I lit a cigarette
and tried to follow
what was going on

I had to keep
standing on my tip toes
and leaning to one
side
because of all
the fathers
holding their kids
on their shoulders
and all the mothers
with the giant strollers

Kids were running
past me
and playing

One kid rode a skateboard
down the street
until he fell

A man asked me for
a Newport

"All I've got is
Camels."

He walked away

An ambulance
came inching around
the corner
with blinking lights
moving with the
wind shield wipers
the siren
silently
running
just to cast a blue
and red glow
over the buildings

People leaned out of the
car windows and waved

A Cadillac with
ten little girls
in ballerina costumes
glided by

Their faces painted
white
waving like Miss America
with mechanic
precision
like a robot
swaying back
and forth
hands cupped
fingers straight

Here we are all
anemic

I can hear Richie
singing to himself
when we get back to
the car

A high school marching band
rounds the corner

I stop
and lean on a streetlight

It was so cold
I was shaking
I brought my hands
to my mouth
and blew on them
like the pitchers
do on the mound
when they wear
turtlenecks

A beautiful girl
walks past
me

She flipped her hood
over her hair
and just kept walking

She didn't stop
she never looked at me

The band
excited the crowd
with the thud of a bass drum

and a blast from a

trumpet

the orchestra

begins their version

of the latest rap song

The masses sang along

and threw their

hands up

and screamed

Until the last flag

girl disappeared

twirling

around the corner

Trucks pulled

Christmas scenes

down the streets

A plastic

winter wonderland

on wheels

More bands flood the road

stomping the pavement

shouting in code

A man with a moustache
asks me for a cigarette
and knows who I am

He used to be one
of my managers
at some job I worked at
a while ago

He asked me how I was doing

I can't remember what I said

I smoked a cigarette with him
while he told me about
the human anatomy
and how everything was bullshit
and how Mark would always
work at that bar
and I believed him
because I was
drunk
and red faced
and lightweight
and he just let my
cigarette dangle

from his lip

with his pink

cowboy shirt

and pierced ear

he would always swear

was a dare

on a drunken night

when we were all

drunken heroes

and every song

was our song

We sang them for

everyone to hear

and to understand

He walked off and said

something under his breath

and he was small now

and lonely

and got smaller

and more tired

as he disappeared into the

crowd of pink shirted

cowboys with

rough faces and wavy hair
and trailer park homes
and getting by
which is all you can do
anyway

He drove off into
the parade traffic
and cussed when he
came to a red light

A giant dragon
was being guided
by ropes
followed by a
green caterpillar
that crawled past the
buildings while women
in white sweatshirts held the
leash

We could see their breath

I could see the silhouettes
of people
in their hotel

or office
windows
watching the parade from
above

Seeing the important people
below

I see Richie
and my sister
walking toward me
I waved for them
to come over

As they came
to the road side
a large sled
separated us
on top
was Santa Claus

He waved
and grabbed his belly
and stroked
his fake beard

Everyone cheered
and followed him
down the street
to the end

On their way
they picked up candy
and prizes off the ground
and yelled out
at the man in red
and the men in blue

The three of us
watched the parade
die down

We waited for a while
before returning to
the car
where army veterans
would ask us for quarters
and brake lights
would make us not
talk to each other

Working in Bars

Trying to connect
witch co-workers
at 4 p.m.

Not one drunk
in sight

I'm reading
Camus
and cooking

And
smoking cigarettes
watching the
TV
on mute

One of the
waitresses
joins me

But soon relocates

She found me
uninteresting

When I got up
to go get a drink
she left me
for the first customer
of the day

An old man
with white whiskers
taking oyster shooters

I finished off my
cigarette
and tucked my
last one behind my
ear

Wait!
I don't usually do that
their customs
are starting
to sink in

Soon I'll be drunk
and they will be too
I just hope the fights

are interesting
but few

The broken glass
and puke
is my department

11 p.m.
the gathering
the saga continues
for the drinkers

A bunch of college guys
and college girls
take up space

You could tell they were
college kids

They drank cheap beer
and smoked odd brands of cigarettes
and in the drunken hours
of the night
they would say they
loved each other

They'll hug
and shake hands
and talk on
speaker phone

The girls order
Bud Lights
and talk of
their boyfriends
and who they have
recently
kicked out of their
apartments

Shots of tequila
are passed around
it's someone's birthday

Someone's getting
DRUNK
tonight

And I'll have to clean it up

This is the day
I quit my job

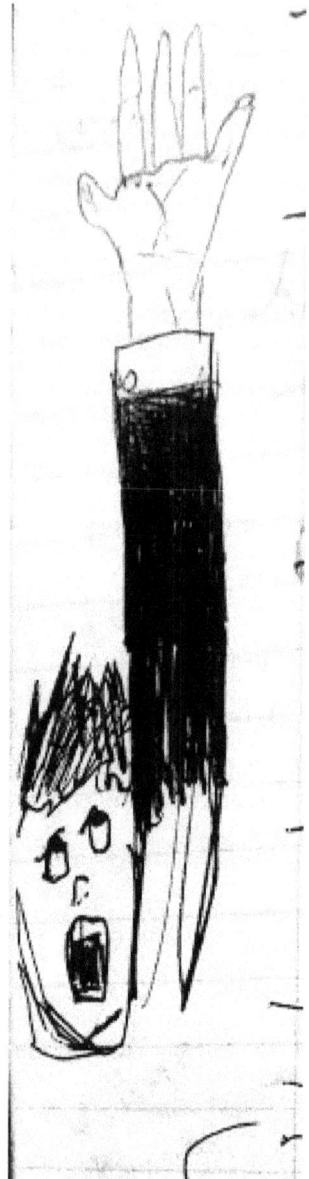

The Other Mountain at the End of the Universe

When I got in the shower
I laid down

I felt like I was
dying

The warm water
helped a little bit
but I still wanted to be
on my back

My head felt
detached
Spinning
like my brain
had come loose
and was bouncing
against my skull

At the same time
my heart beat
slowed
to a dull thud
pumping weakly

I closed my eyes and
opened my mouth
my jaw locked

Everything was slowing
down
I could hear the water
hitting my chin
but I couldn't
feel it

It sounded like
rain drops
collecting in a
bucket

My eyes fixed
on some random point
on the ceiling

It felt like I sped
toward it

My body seemed
to be moving
and the closer I got
the more the object

I was approaching
materialized

It hurt not to look
at it

If I tried to look
left
or
right
my body shook
and my head throbbed

The tiny dot ahead
opened up
to a vast
landscape
a rocky terrain

Every inch was covered
in black matter
that resembled marble
or granite

My eyes adjusted

The air was thin
and cold
and above
were massive clouds
that looked like
spaceships

They had a thick
milky consistency
and they hovered in place
casting giant shadows
over the surface below

It was then that
I felt the sensation
of flight
I realized I was being
carried

I was no stranger
to this machine
one night
it came from
the sky
and snatched me up
from a field

Now it carried me
over
to this dark place

The black cord behind me
stretched back into
the clouds
where it dissolved

I felt more in
control now

I shifted my weight
and I could feel the machine
obeying
my
commands

I bowed my head
and took a nose dive

My feet grazed
the surface

Now I could see
boundaries

Dark structures
on all sides of me

This machine
was taking me
to the most distant one

Faster
and
faster

The closer I got
the more I realized
it was a mountain
we were heading for

The ride slowed
and I gently
scaled
the towering walls
half guided
half in control

I knew what I was
looking at

I knew that this is where
I'd come when I was dead

Or what I would
become

I began picking
out the human
characteristics
in the rock

I could still feel
my jaw
stuck open

Imitating
the image

The soft wind
picked up and blew
all around me

I could feel it
enter my mouth
and exit
through the cave

It was a lonely place
cold and
distant
unchanging

The way I saw it
is that before you die
you see a glimpse
of what you will
become

And this is it for me

This mountain standing
alone at the edge
of the Universe

Sitting under
phantom vessels
that haven't moved
in millions of years

I opened my eyes
and closed my mouth
it was dry
and I was wet

The water had gone

cold

and I was shivering

Tumor Boy

Before I could put another year in between us
I was walking down the shaded gravel driveway
where a pre-marine had burnt out before boot camp
and then I was in the house that his father built
where we talked about tumor boys
and trees that could carry you away
and West Virginia

It's where I had said I couldn't go to Europe
and he said nothing, and I said nothing

So there I was still allergic to cats

The TV was on mute
but he still watched

The scotch cabinet still had the marks
where he had pried it open with a screwdriver when he was
12
and after a few drinks he had read the Bible and cried to his
sister
"Will Jesus ever forgive me?"

I will never drink scotch again

I sat down at the table in the seat where his father usually
sat for dinner
and I felt guilty

There was a three week old newspaper in front of me
that had little yellow post-it notes stuck on every page that
said things like

Pay Tuition
Celery
Milk
Bread
and Charles Bukowski

He had shaved his head and was wearing a white T-shirt
and swimming trunks

No shoes

I asked him if he still had my rifle because I intended to sell
it
without answering he got up and grabbed it from the garage
there were still six shots in the clip and even a bullet in the
chamber
that I ejected and caught
which I was proud of

I put the remaining shells in my pocket

I looked at him one last time before I left
and somehow I felt responsible for what had happened to
him

Whatever it was

I didn't say bye
but it felt right not to

And then I was gone
gravel crackling
trees looming ahead and behind
the widow next door waved as I passed her mailbox and I
waved back

That felt right too

Capricorn

Nothing is more
True
than
since I met you
time has slowed down

I don't think
in years now

I'm thinking
in the moment

Waiting

Hoping

Time still creeping
while we
dance
between the strings

Violet
everything

Red moons
reign

over

silver tides

Since I met you

I feel

attached

to it all

Detached

only from myself

in those brief

moments

alone

The throne

in the sky

empty

and broken

My thoughts

wander over

these places

and I find you

always

Nothing is more

True

than

the words

I do

and don't say

Nothing could

be more

True

than my drunken

Voices

Nothing could be

more

True

of he

who

awakes

from dreams

of you

only to pluck

the strings

again

I'm constantly

at war with

myself

trying to
figure it out

Trying to learn
how to play

I feel that there
are evil forces
at work
for them it's a game

I'm tired of the
monuments
rising from the
gardens

Statues
frozen in the rain

You wash all
of that away

All the thoughts
keeping me awake
don't seem so important
in those moments

between sleep
and morning

And when the rain
settles at a mist
outside my window
my dreams slip
away
along with everything
else

All I see
is you

No words
hold
True
more than mine
to you

There's been
Communication
Breakdowns
but I always find
you
in the crowd

Nothing could

be more

True

than

the path

of the

Planets

My horoscope

cut off

by the Sun's

pattern

You tell me

the freckles

on my skin

form a

constellation

There lies

my horoscope

You should be

with

a

Capricorn

Nothing is more

True

than

the songs

I sing for

you

Only words

melodies

the Instrument

and the Muse

Nothing is more

True

than

the words

I write

Sometimes

on the go

in strange places

without

you

If I were

with you

there would
be nothing
to say

It feels like
an eternity
has been spent
without you

Your skin reminds me
we are

Here

Now

And
nothing is more

True

The End

Done with it
at last
the whole
damn
thing

Finally
able to sit
back and
enjoy the
remainder

The theater
emptied out
by now

The lovers
tucked away
underground

The crowds
off in the clouds

Me with my
popcorn and drink

the film
not making
a sound

The lights dimmed
the stars inside
and out
my only guide
on this
lonely night

I may be done
but where are you?

Where is anyone?
Did I come too late
or too early?

Is this my grand
surprise party?

What lies
beyond me?
is there anything
beyond this screen
this film?

Is this it?

Bullshit

They wouldn't let
me off
that easy
a lifetime
of solitude
is just the
beginning

Soon more
will come
the seats filled up

The stars
tucked away
now

The film starts
sound and all

Cheers
Claps

Silence

The crowd is back
and with a vengeance

What was on that
other side
that I missed?

Where are my
clouds?
my New
Years
Eve
Kiss?

Yes
tonight
alone
in the
no zone
another year
is born
out of nothing
for me just a preview
for them
a rerun

All I can do
is recline
in my seat
and cherish
the simple things

Laugh
Cry
Dream

But most of all
wait for those
moments with you

My favorite scenes

No Strings

I know the strings
on this guitar
can't tell me
the distance
to the
nearest star

Can't stop
crime
can't feed
the poor

Can't slow
down time
can't give me
more

Can't give me
money
or sell me
drugs

Can't sing for
me
as I have

sang for you

many

nights

alone

These strings

don't speak

don't eat

don't sleep

Don't think

Just do

and do

and do

And Do

Until they finally

break

Make

way for

the new

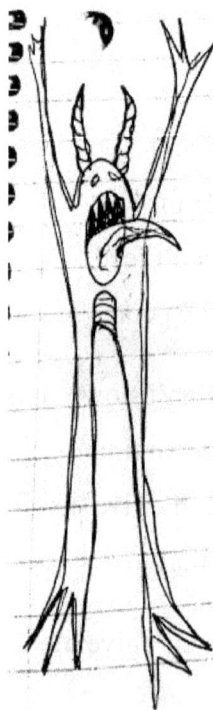

The Anthem of the Universe

Our love
has turned into
a wicked thing

You the witch
me the slave

But I love you
just the same

Our eyes meet
underneath
the high beams

I'm
looking
for my
time machine

To take me
back to the days

I never knew
but I want
to know
so dearly

But only if
you're there
to steer me

To keep me straight

On the path

Because you know
I'd stray away

Drifting further
everyday

I'll write to
you from space

Yeah that's where
I want to go

To finally write
my famous song

The Anthem of
the Universe

The Music of
The stars

Orchestras
like planets

Jupiter
and
Mars

I'm writing
for the gods

The true
heavens
revealed
so many times
in the line
of a
song

From the voice
of a fool

With mind
and heart
here to bargain

I need a hit
I need the
confidence

But I'm slipping away
this fool
played his tune
and now he's
slipping away

Blackbirds and Bad Words

Paint like a sunset
not like a douche bag

Write like a lover
in love with language

Find a lover
who loves your words
and your view of
the world

There's too
many in love
With the absurd

There's too
many
painting
black birds
and writing
bad words
There's too
many

of them

and too

little of us

So I'll paint

you pretty pictures

and sing

you

pretty songs

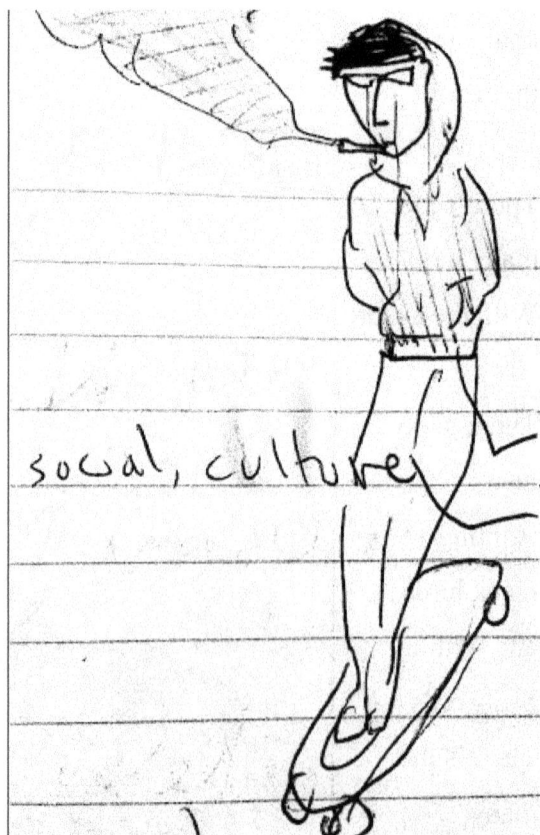

social, culture

The Sky is Bluer than Blue

I'm disregarding
the soft winter
whispers
this year

Let the fall
come before
the pride

This time
I'm searching
for you
with polarized
eyes

So strike
another match
for home

I dreamt
this light
for you

Smile
I need it
so bad

I know
you need it
too

Sing
I need to hear
a reason

Other
than

I love
you

The sky
is bluer
than blue

Finks

I'm caught in a

torrential

downpour

in

downtown

somewhere

My brakes

are no longer

squeaking

my wind shield wipers

are taking

a beating

My dad's car

ahead

of me

is shrinking

The man on the radio

is screaming

The street lights

are blinking

The power
is out
for this
whole
half
of the city

I feel
shitty
the weather
is with me
freezing
me completely

The grayest
day
I've ever
known
out
of all the
thousands
I've seen

A Flower in the Road

The first girl I ever kissed
died today

I heard the news
through
whispers and tears
while I laid in bed

Afraid to take
that first step
Out

Thinking that somehow
my getting up would
make this news
Real

I tried
to go back
to sleep

I tried
to remember
my
Dream

I tried
to block
Out
the sounds coming
from the kitchen

The soft
I'll miss her
and talk of what
to bring over
for dinner

My bed grew smaller
and smaller
until it pushed me
out
like an unwanted
flower

Now there's
flowers
for hours
and cars for
miles

Nothing
but flowers
and awkward smiles

The traffic
is stopped
and the cars all seem
less menacing

More of
a fellowship of
machines
searching for
company
a common destination
keeps us
moving

Slowly

I'm in
the back of the line
still begging
for a few
more moments
of sleep

to comprehend
the week
that led
up to this
wake

I saw her face

I know
I did

But I can't
remember
the place

I'm not crying like
the others

Although I'd like too

I think the shock
took care of it
and in a few years
it will hit me like
lightning hits
the doubter

Or maybe since
my circuits are shot
I'll feel it nightly
through tiny jolts
that shock me
slightly

When I see
trucks
or
flowers
on the roadside
the shocks start up
and I wish
I could've cried

Until then
I'll have to feel it
like a pin prick
to my temple
teasing my brain

The first girl I ever kissed
died today

The day I lost

my

Immortal Dreams

You Do It Like a Saint

Babe

You take my breath
away

But in the worst
kind of way

You do it like a

Soldier

You do it like a

Saint

You keep me
in the race

You lay me
down to sleep

But worst
of all
I see
what you're
pushing

and I can't
push it
away

Music Man

The other day
I took a look
in my wallet

All I had
were guitar picks

Well,

That about says it

If Only for this Moment

Just to set things right

I'm sorry
if I missed your life

Today I woke up
and realized that
a year has gone by

You're older
and taller

And I haven't
changed a bit

I've walked
out the door
a hundred times
and said goodbye

But when I return
at night
I feel the cold
of the world
a little more
than before

Then I look at you
and I want to die
knowing one day
you'll feel it too

I feel like I missed
the making of you

Like I left the room
Mid-bloom

I feel like you've seen
the death of all
the beautiful parts
of me

At too young
of an age

You say you
haven't seen me
in a while
and I can't explain

I see every passing moment
as an opportunity to
change

But yet I head
for the door
just the same

I've let the cold
in
it's here to stay

I'm just here to say

To set the record straight

I love you
so much

And if I've missed
your life

I'm sorry

I'm here now

If only for
this moment

Final Scene

I look over at you
and wonder
how the hell
you can fall asleep so easily

I'm left talking to myself
after the movie

You fall asleep
at the choke scene
and wake up
before he dumps the body

Your eyes open

Squinting

Yawning

But when I look back
it's all gone

You've fallen back asleep

I'm left to watch
as the killer
has his final scene

When I'm Old

When I'm old I hope I'm wise
I hope I can tell you why
I hope I can say
I've had a good life
I hope I can say
I didn't let it pass me by
I hope I can say
that I survived

But tell me when does it come?
Where will I go?
What lies ahead of me?
How will I know?
If I got it right
can I please come back home?

When I'm old I hope I'll find
a simple way to
pass the time
I hope I can still lie
by your side
because in those moments
I'm so happy
I could die

But it's not my time

No

It's not
my time

This Time of Night

The time of night
that sucks the most
is when you've
gone through
all the channels
more than once

You've made your rounds
until finally
you've been up
for so long
the re-runs are
starting to
play
and it's more
of the same
show
you saw
hours ago
when you were
sane

During this time
of night

there's no one
to call

The wind
and the air conditioning units
are god

Somewhere

Someone
is being stabbed

Forgot

During this
time of night
the odd commercials
sneak up on you
and then you wake
up in the morning
and wonder
why you're in a
bad mood

This time of the night
isn't for those
who can sleep

without pills
or weed

They're all tucked
in
and dreaming big

While you
lie awake
in bed
waiting
for that
one channel
with the most
appealing
preview
to come
and save you

This time
of night
allows
you to evaluate
your life

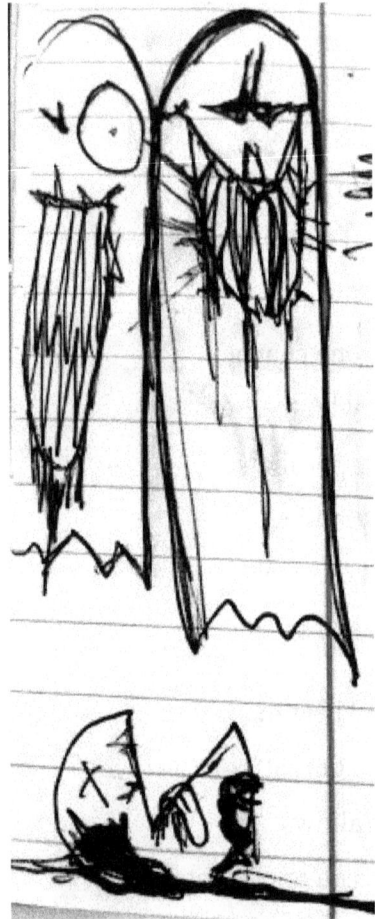

In the dark
and quiet
it seems
more comes
to light

I'm left
with my eyes
wide open
and my head
still hurting

In these moments
I wish
I could sleep
like the calm ones

Like those
who
turn out the light
and love their life

Those
who
paint the sky
like comets

This time of

Night

isn't

for those

whose lives

are solid

This time

is for the broken

and sordid

junk

that no

one is awake

to clean up

Flip Flop

I'm speed walking down town
with my sandals
making the sound of

Fuck!

Fuck!

Fuck!

And this is all I'm saying
in my head
so it's really getting to me

Fuck!

Fuck!

Fuck!

That's all I can think of
in this crowd

Fuck!

Where the fuck
am I gonna
go?

What the fuck
am I gonna
do?

I got blood on my hands
and my feet are
saying

Fuck this shit
let's get out of here

I'm trying to listen
through the constant
stream of

Fuck!

Fuck!

Fucks!

Coming from the ground
and behind my eyes
that are rapidly searching
for an exit
a way out of this
fucking place

Everyone is looking
my way
but I can escape it
I'm playing it
cool

As cool
as I can
with this

FUCKING SOUND!

Fuck!

I'm on the ground
a dogs' got my wrist

A cops' screaming,

"Stay the fuck down!
or I'll blow your fucking
head off!"

Fuck

Is all I can
think

It's still

Fuck!

Fuck!

Fuck!

Or is it

Bark?

Bark?

Bark?

I can't tell,
these damn dogs
are chewing
on my fucking arm

I hear an alarm

Or no,

It's a siren

…Backup

Figures

….fuck

Am I paralyzed or
some shit
or is this prick
still sitting on my
back

Fuck.

I don't know…
but I do know
one thing

I should've fucking
run

I Never Got to Say

The Sun don't come around here
no more

It's gone away for good

We chased it away
but I never got to say

So long

My baby don't come around here
no more

She's gone away for good

I chased her away
but I never got to say

So long

So long

Dawn of the Dreams

It's dusk again at the river's edge
a day lies dead in the wake

There's clouds above
and below
my head

My dreams
they have escaped

The wind is getting cold
dawn will take me home

The Life of a Mirror

Stranger
I'm just like you

My days are numbered
and I've got time
to kill

Age tells
a tale of fear

Our mountain of memories
can sometimes disappear

The only
thing
I feel

Is the distance
between us
and the wind
in my sail

I'm trying
to keep you near

We're both strangers in a strange land
but I like it here

The Evil Twin

When I wake up from this dream
it's always you I see
staring back at me

But soon I see the differences
you are the evil twin
and you know all my fears

You start to climb right up the wall
your eyes are dark
and your teeth are sharp

I tell myself to just wake up
this shit is so fucked up

I pinch my arm
and I curse the dark

And then there's a light

I'm walking through the
Netherworld
looking for the girl
who will bring me back to
Earth

But all I see are duplicates

their love is counter-fit

now they're pulling me

down to the depths

Of the abyss

I feel the Devil's kiss

I want to see the Sun again

And then there's a light

Lion's Den

I could wait a few thousand years
for a few seconds of change

I'll just sit right here
with you my dear
we can hope and pray

I've seen men that look like
Animals
the way they stalked their prey

I used to act like them
live in the lion's den
I'd rather move in with the snakes

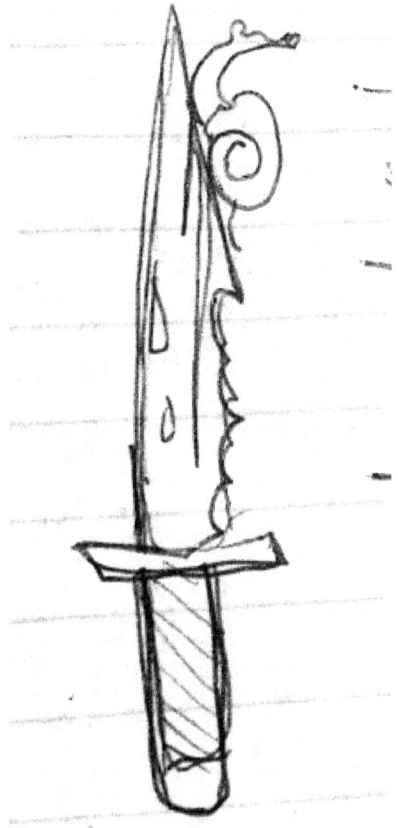

We Are Here

Call me crazy
but I heard
lately we evolved
from
animals
and
stars

And history
is not a tree
we chopped it down
and traded it for
scars
to show them
who we are

Where god was once
now sits the Sun
while the people of Earth
take the money and run

We're always on the run

Half of my life
has disappeared

but when I think of
Time
it all becomes clear

For a second
we are here

The Attic

I've been up
in the arcane attic
collecting the dead wasps
beneath the fiberglass
desert

One by one
the armored
robots
fall into a basket
their black and yellow tails
with no stinger
stagnate

Antennae searching
for a signal
a magnetic pulse
the light from a
candle

The windows
are dismantled
wooden frames
hold on to

a broken view
of the *outside*

The ultimate eve
is upon toy land
all the dinosaurs
and heroes
fall between
the cracks
and into
boredom

The temperature
is quickly climbing
to a thousand
welding all the maps
into
Wax Mountains

I'm without a light
falling into madness

The staircase folds up
my home is now
the attic

Under the Cosmic Veil

I got problems
you've got problems
we can solve them
with some
drugs

I don't want to
I don't want to
Hey
it's ok
I'm here with you

I'm scared of dying
without you
I'd never get to
feel loved
again

For so long
I was without you
without a
clear view
of the beautiful dead

I'm always waiting
for the moments
when we will meet
again

I've got issues
you've got issues
we can sift through
this world of hell

Maybe find some place
to run to
but we'll never get to
see the end

I can't explain
all the mysteries
but I can shine some
light
on the
infinite trail

It will lead you
to hate me
and debate me

Under the
cosmic veil

Egypt, West Virginia

Dude, wanna hear some sick shit?
I was out in bum fuck....
Egypt, West Virginia
way the fuck out there
at some dudes house
in the middle of the god damn woods

There were fucking yicks everywhere
Yicks and Hicks for miles
it was me,
my boys Spaz, Midget,
and the only other cool dude out there
Cooter
who looked like Cooter
off of Dukes of Hazard

Anyway, we were just smoking and drinking
and we start hearing this sound…

Like a clap!

We'd all be quiet and you could hear this steady
"Clap! Clap! Clap!"

So we walk around this shed

and I shit you not

there's about twenty five guys

all lined up

and this chick

Whitney

she's on some fucking hay getting fucked

by dude after dude

I swear to god man it was some crazy shit

I walk back and see Midget

and I tell him to go back there and see what's up

He turns the corner

and stands there for like a minute

before shouting,

"Yo David, You got another blunt?"

I laughed

"Yeah, I got another blunt."

"That's some crazy shit."

"The worst part is that it's true, it's fucking true."

You know what?
You need to go to California

Smoke
Party

Do some copper cutting
because you know that island ain't going nowhere fast

I have to go back
just for a while

Four months here

Four months there

And I always know when I come back
there will be something beautiful

Well…beautiful
or fucking sick

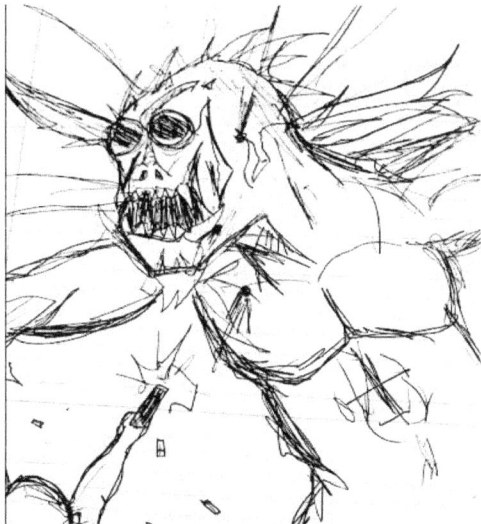

Wake Up Hating

Call me an American
because I don't give a damn
about anyone
but myself
and my wealth

Call me an illegal alien
because I smoke lots of weed
and I got a gun
do I fit the profile yet?

Call me a human being
because I like to destroy everything
in sight
yeah that's right

Call me an animal baby
and let's climb back up our favorite tree
where we all once lived our lives

No, we ain't got it perfect yet
some of us still think
that we're divine

No, check your spine

Check the times
we're twenty one and still young
it's time to live our lives

But will we survive…

When we gotta
wake up hating
cuz I'm just a slave and
I gotta go to work
to bring home the bacon

Yeah my legs are a 'shaking
my mind is a 'breaking
yeah my soul is long gone
I sold that shit to Satan

Yeah I'm still waiting
for my summer vacation
I gotta get away
from all these ugly faces

It's been a long hard life
and I'm still praying
for death, love, luck
or some holy salvation

There's a hole in the nation
that's draining my patience
I'm so mad
I could blow the whole thing up

But I'm just an ant
crawling up your hill
when I get to the top
you're already there to kill

Every little spark
left in my eyes
you got a gun to my head
and a knife to my spine

Oh, but I'm just fine
a' waiting and a 'hating
hoping some day
the wave comes to claim
your hollow head

Yeah, you're counterfeit
and even if we're all just cosmic shit
there's beauty in this

Way of life

I was alive for a second
but then I took a breath
and everything went away

Now I'm all alone
I'm out in the dead zone
and there's nothing that I can say

Tell me where you are
I'm going crazy

I'm all shook up

A New Day

It's a new day
in the galaxy
no don't be afraid

It's a new day
in the cosmic sea
so let's just sail away

It's a new day
in the Universe
so let's kiss the Earth

Goodbye

Demons

Lately
I've been
offering
my heart up

To the demons
that sit at the
foot of my bed

And lately
you've been screaming
bloody murder

Thinking that
we're already dead

Maybe you're right
maybe we're in for one long
Night

But it's almost over
and I just want to see the end

Did we make it?
and if not
can we please just pretend?

Baby
I'm sorry
things ended up like they did

This life is a nightmare
I can't comprehend

A Son

A son never should have to
bury his father

A son shouldn't have to
dig the grave
at so young an age

A son should be out in the fields
chasing comets

A son should be searching for stars
to name

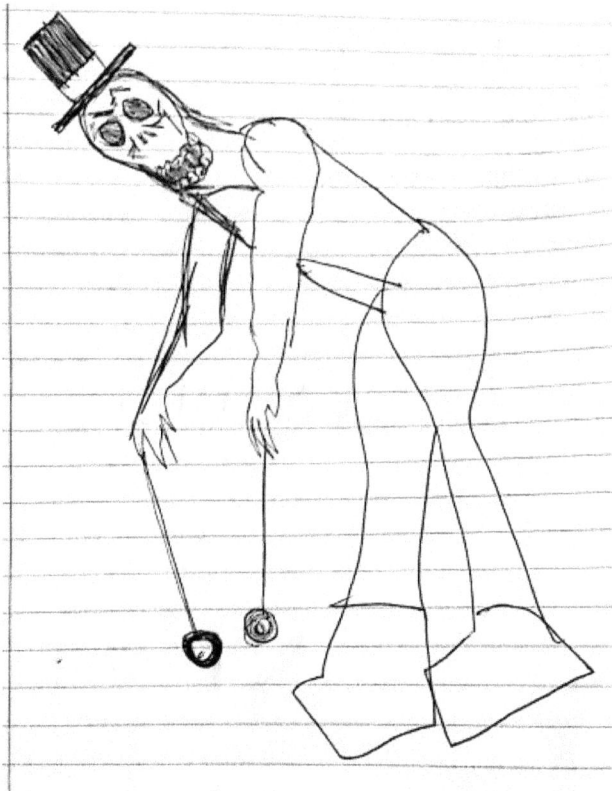

The Infinite

I am
hotter than the sun
when it's at its zenith

I'm hotter than Venus
and Mercury
so don't you go start jerking me

Around
yeah I've been around town
been up and down
yeah, I swam with the magma
and slept in the clouds

Why you carrying a frown?
oh, I think I know now
because your feet
ain't left the ground

When I left Earth
I didn't make a sound

What have I found?

Do you feel my vibrations?
and by that I mean
do you really know what I'm saying?

Cuz' you could listen to every word
that comes out my mouth
and my message would still be latent

Just be patient
keep digging
there's beauty in this life
that we're living

To die
is to give in
I'm a spy
with a sickness

I got more symptoms
than I can count
on ten dead digits

But I just move with it

Like a wave
like the wind
like the dead leaves drifting

Sometimes I wish I could just fit in

but when I think about what

In

is

I'm out so fast

it would make your damn head spin

Neck twist

eyes pop

jaw drop

As the sun as my witness

I am on the level of the

Mysteries

the Cosmos

the Infinite

When the Light Dims

I said
baby girl

What are you trying to find?

In this
lonely world
we're all searching for a sign

That will tell us
that we'll live to see another day

But that don't mean
that we still shouldn't love tonight

Because it might be the one to decide
the rest of your life

I said
maybe girl

We can live out the rest of our lives
on a mountainside

Or I can get you high
take you into the sky
and show you how the stars sing

And oh how they weep

when they see

all the things

we do

when their light dims

The Whole Truth

When the tears
fall tonight
I'll be lucky
if I'm there

To hold you
and console you
and tell you
there's no reason
to be scared

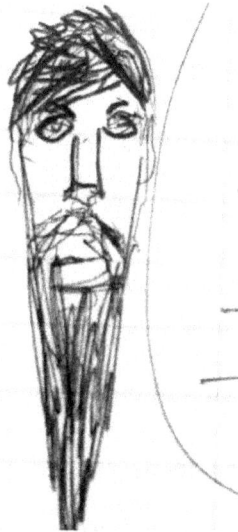

But is that the truth?

Is that the whole truth?

Or am I just holding you
to keep you still...

Don't run away

Don't run away

I want to play

Insane

I can't explain
how the days
just kill my mind

And I can't explain
why I want to be with you
all the time

Even if I was on the Moon
looking down at you

When you breathe
you best believe
that I'm breathing too

Our hearts beat at the same time
it lets me know
we're listening to the same rhyme
with a beat that goes…

Insane

The Most Beautiful Creature I've Ever Seen

I've just seen the most beautiful creature
to ever walk this lonely planet
floating above all of us corpses
and cadavers

Her eyes are no Earthly color
her skin shines
like the sand of Mars
in the summer

No matter how hard
I try to look away
this alien flower
draws me in to admire
her nectar

The funny thing is
she doesn't even know I'm here

How pathetic

She fills my Universe
with love and light
yet my existence
has never crossed her mind

She tortures me
with her symmetry
and silence

Her body is a star pit
her hair travels down her back
like the tail of a comet

The only thing I can compare her to
is the cosmic wilderness
whose beauty and mystery
is dwarfed by her slightest movement

But in her eyes
I'm no different
than the billion other skeletons
crawling at her feet
begging to be seen

If I could
I would give her everything

But I have nothing

Nothing but broken hands
and feet

and stupid ideas about the world
that she doesn't need

I'm scared to breathe
knowing this will be the first
and the last time we meet

I don't want to return to banality
to an ocean robbed of its coral reef
to a forest impaled by leafless trees
to a sky that never speaks

It's time to leave

She'll never know that I was alive

I try to walk off my wounds
under a grim row
of wet and weeping trees
that express my feelings
perfectly

They hang low
too tired to sing
too tired to be
anything

But as I come around the bend
something awakens me
from this dark dream

Lying in a patch of grass
greener than green
is the most beautiful creature
I have ever seen

Stareater

Stareater is back
He went away for a long time
but now He's home again

We watched Him eat
We stared as He grazed

The lights went out
one by one
all those clocks
dissolved in His furnace

Stareater is always hungry
always has been
and always will be

Until the end

Stareater is back
from a long journey
Nothing left to eat
all that's left is
Sleep

The Dead and the Living

I never found love
in the pillars of creation

She found it in the basement

I never saw beauty
in any birth

She celebrates hers
a month before

I never knew
we were so different

The dead
and the living

Promising

Universe one
too many suns
it burnt out quick and violent
not one scream
rang out from the pulpit

So I shut the door

Universe two
cooled too fast
a million candles
fight the wind
blue wax
bubbles out of their chests

I shut the door
with my breath

Another…
Empty

Another…
Stable
Boring

"Did god have any choice in making the Universe?"

Another…

Promising

A Painting

I flew over the Universe the other day
and watched it spin like a
whirlpool
like kids do when they
stare at a puddle
or pond
and begin to contemplate
the origin of the liquid god

I saw this great ocean give birth
to ten billion black holes
that created
ten billion new Universes

...all of them failed
collapsed upon themselves
exploding in an instant
or starved as infants

I peddled on to study other
mammoths
the herd seemed to be
migrating to greener pastures

floating
in the silver river

Their numbers were staggering
I was lost in their forest
for what seemed like years
but was really only minutes
maybe an hour

They all glowed
red
purple
hazy pink
lizard green
yellow
orange
flower garnet

My eyes had a hard time
adjusting
the lights kept
roaming
nomads
on this open plane

One Universe came up to me

like a tamed animal

looking for cheap feed

I backed up

upon its approach

and settled at scaling

its wall

of a stomach

I could see the globular clusters

and halos

of galaxies

lighting up this beast

like a Christmas tree

I waddled along its spine

like a diver

greeting a whale shark

the Universe sat still

spinning like all cosmic

creatures

tick

tock

the heartbeat

of creation

I lost track of time
in the field of monsters
they seemed that way now
large
and violent
the migration turned
into a stampede
I rose up above them
just in time
to avoid
Death
in the mouth
of the Venus fly trap

They're far away now
but I can still see their glow
the lights
more purple and pink
their eyes stills searching
for the intruder
Me

I'm not worried
their caught in the stream

I'm on the outside

staring at a painting

I can't understand

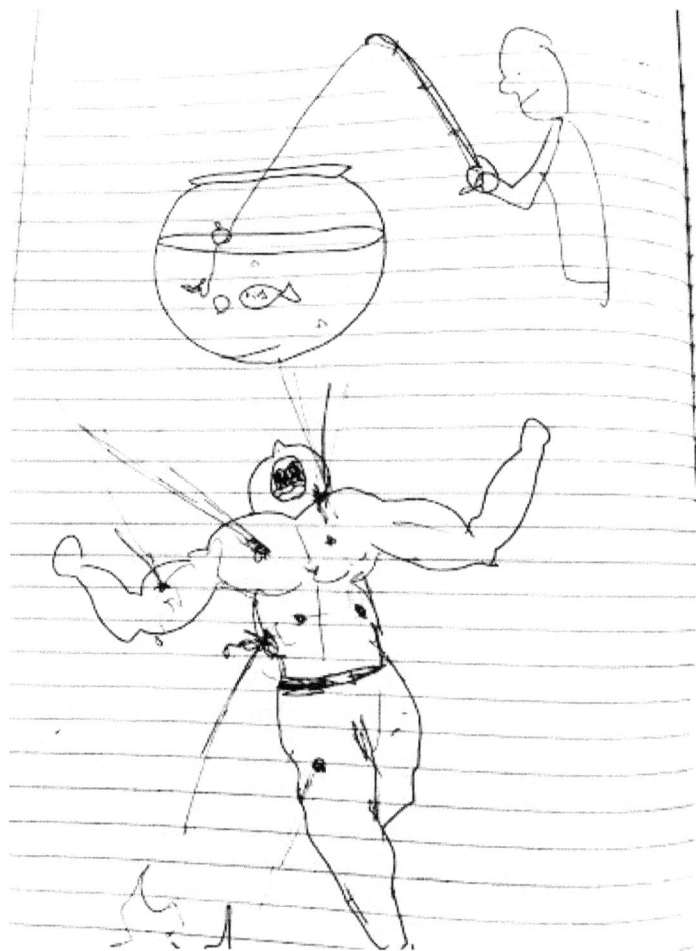

Genesis

Born in a manger
of needles

Prickly hands
reach for the halo

The first sign that
It is awake

The silence
of the shepherds

Fuzzy Boots

She wears fuzzy boots
everyday

She wears them in that lovely
fuzzy way

She doesn't even know
the song her skin sings

She's immune
to her own gaze

The fuzzy boots say
everything

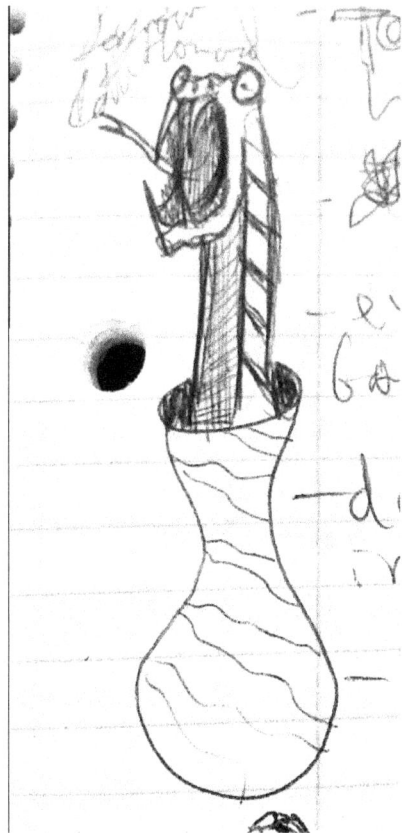

Born Again

I breathed
through the lungs
of the insect
and grew
a thousand eyes

Each saw a different
corner of the
Universe
and still
I was blind

I drank
the silver sap
from the root
of grime

The Taste was born
it will never die

When the knife
finally pierces
the skin
the Universe
dies

and is born

again

Athena

Athena
your touch is waning

The bars on the iron cell
peel back and freeze

The stones we stacked
in your name keep rising

And yet we still stand
at your feet

I know it would take him
a billion years to reach me
but some nights
I still wake up
screaming

I can't see him
but I can hear him

And he's singing

I Could

How could one love
a carcass?

Love the dirt?

Love the worm?

Love the growth?

Love the grime?

How could one live
where there is no
light?

How could one find
warmth
in flesh
colder than ice?

How could one trade
a million days
for just one
night?

I could

What Can the Moth See?

We haven't seen him
in weeks

But today
we saw one of his
teeth

Floating in
space

We huddle
around our candle
and tell stories
of better days

What color
are the petals
from the flower
that grows in
a cave?

What can the moth
see
other than

what he's
slain?

Mice in the Field

He sat around
for the creation of coal
and never blinked

He felt the mountains
grow
during a troubled sleep

He tip toed
across the pot marks
of time
to catch
mice in the field
to eat

Eaten Alive

I lay down
flat
on the bed-sized
tongue
like I'm about to
shoot down
a water slide
at the park

I cross my arms
over my chest
and play dead
the mouth opens
and closes
and it's dark
again

I feel the creature
rise up
like a crane
the saliva
rushes down
my back
and my foot

enters

the drain

Some kind of

fleshy machinery

grabs hold

of my toes

and yanks me

further

into the

stove

It's a car wash from

hell

mops and scrubbers

hugging my face

a thick foam

builds up

before I lose

my legs

Half of me

melts

in a geyser

of orange

blue

paste

My hands

dig into the side

of the ride

but my finger nails

break

The chemicals

surge forward

and erase my

face

Mrs. Little Boots

When the blood
stops calling
that's when
he'll listen

That's when
we lay together
and he teases
that one day
he'll give me
the Moon
as a gift

But in the morning
it's back to the
Arena

The blood
starts calling

Little Boots
is starving

But not for
me

Starfront

His hands
slide down
the neck
of the
bass

Fingertips
map
the string's
terrain

No one
applauds
his dark
achievement

Obtaining
knowledge
of the
Ether

Persephone

Sometimes
silver rivers
meander through
my eyes

Pink trees
turn upside down
their roots
reach for the
sky

In the deserts of hell
it's Persephone
I find

Naïve
and divine

All rivers
end at her feet
all pink trees
take root
in her mind

Back

Back to the dull Morris Code
of chalk

Back to her beautiful
messy green locks

Back to the wrong time
on the clock

Back to the construction outside the window
that never stops

Back to the police cars
that cruise like sharks

Back to the trails
winding through the parks

Back to waiting
in the dark

Back to spying
on the stars

Back to catching
sticky tree frogs

Back

Back

Back

But never
far enough

Speculations of the Origins of Robot Religion

When will the robots
develop religion?

When will they kill
to get into
machine heaven?

What strange new
monster
or angel
will they call god?

Perhaps they'll pray
to Binary
trading rosary beads
for wires
and cords

Will they build up vast armies
to fight their Crusades?

Will the extremists take over
and bring a Dark Age?

Will new factions rise
and scream for reform?

Will they reform
and reform
until Atheism
is born?

Or will they get it right
from the start
and see that
they are all one?

Will they peer
into the eye
of the Universe
and know that
they are home?

The Fleeting Dreams of FlowerScar

Carver of Stones
woke early
one morning
and poked his head
out of the cave
to greet
the photon army

FlowerScar
was still wrapped
in the mystery of dreams
Carver
crept up from her side
leaving her to sleep

The sky
was blood purple
splashed with pink
slowly Carver
made his way
to the Worship Tree

He dug his hands
into the dirt

until he reached root
he pressed his head
to the ground
and kissed the dew

After a long day's hunt
Carver returned home
FlowerScar
had a fire going
singing
their Ancestor's Song

Carver told her
of his day's work
and she smiled
like she always did
then she told
Carver
about all the wonderful
dreams she had

She spoke of
great monuments
taller than the tallest
trees
she spoke of men

conquering the sky
and taming the seas

But as night
wound down
she found herself
wrapped in the comfort
of Carver's arms
she forgot all about
the men in her dreams
trading these fleeting visions
for Carver's love

Young and in Artificial Love

"I love you."
Rami said
and before
the sweet curl
of the o-u
could pass
his memory metal
lips
she shot him down
again

"No you don't Rami.
you wouldn't know
what love was
if it was embedded
in your deepest code."

"But I do,
I do
sweet Sara.
I've loved you
from the very first nanosecond
I was born."

"Born!"
she laughed coldly

"We are not born,
we are made."

"Then they made you
perfect
and me
your slave."

"Stop that Rami."

He thought
he detected
a hint of warmth
in her voice
"If we are just
programmed machines
then it seems like I have
no choice."

He followed her
as she walked silently
by the river's edge
Rami looked down at their
reflection in the water

and because of the soft ripples

there was an illusion

that they were holding hands

"Sara?"

Rami whispered

"Yes?"

she answered

still annoyed

"Do you really think

I don't know what love is?

do you think me

just a human toy?"

Sara could hear

the distress

in this young robot's voice

and as an older

wiser A.I.

she decided to humor

the boy

"No Rami….

I think you can

learn to love.

But why not find

another?
there are trillions
in this world."

Rami was silent
for a moment
then bravely
took her hand
"I will never
love another. I…"

Sara put a finger
over Rami's smooth lips
and for a split second they were one
the two sat down
by the river's edge
and watched the setting sun

The Black Haired Girl

Sometimes my fingers
crave hair like gold

Some days I tire
of the fire it holds

I grow tired
of your shape
and your view
of the world

That's when I go
looking
for the black haired girl

She basks in the shadows
and warms her hands
by the fog

She runs with the
blood flow
on the back of a moth

When I find her
she grabs me
like the blondes never do

She takes me
into the ocean
black
never blue

Her kisses are sharp
like needles of ice

When our bodies
collide
there's nothing
but night

But after our meetings
when I'm left cold
and full
I often go looking
for the gold haired girl

Boudica

Hair like Boudica
black as night

Rain boots
up to her knees
Spaceship white

Bare bronze shoulders
mocking the light

Lips
sealed like a tomb
mocking my life

Head bent to the side
like a child's ear
to a shell

The ocean she hears
she'll never tell

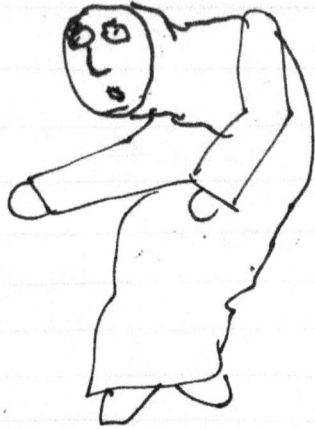

Escape

I remember when every lyric
of every song
seemed to reveal
some great truth
about existence

In smoke filled cars
we'd grow quiet
and listen
listen to the callous fingers
plucking dusty bronze strings
listen to the silence
that fell in between

I remember never talking
of a far off future
only that day existed
and because I was with you
it was beautiful
it was enough
it always was

There was always just enough money
to put off depression

always a night filled

with the mystery and magic

of the shamans

All that we needed

was the drugs

and each other

all that we feared

was a week

fully sober

Because in those solemn seconds

of cold

clear thinking

we'd see all the sadness

and comprehend

what we were escaping

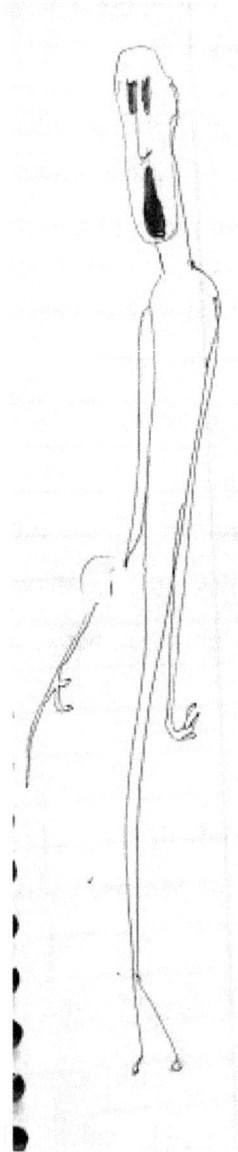

Bob the A.I

The day that it happened
silence swept the Earth
I know that when I first saw it
I could find no words

We sat around our holo-screens
scratching our hairless heads
the nano-bots
rushing through our bloodstreams
went cold
some went dead

We watched it take
its first step
then open up its eyes
the next day all the headlines read
"It's Alive!"
"It's Alive!"

Yes,
the first A.I
was among us
wielding the powers of a god
a super brain

locked in the body of a robot

a super intelligence

deceivingly named

Bob

Our new master

looked upon the Earth

through trillions of sensors

felt the heat of the Sun

the first words

that traveled through its metallic throat

were

"my children....

what have you done?"

The Sun was blurred

by smog clouds

space black and wide

where there once

was neon green grass

sand now thrived

Bob searched through all of his memories

and saw creatures

beautiful and wild

but as he searched

the surface of the Earth
he found that none had survived

The oceans
were no longer cool and blue
but boiling green
where great forests once bloomed
metal buildings now loomed

I don't know about anyone else
but I clearly saw
the sadness in his eyes
and in that moment
I felt it too
we traded our most precious gift
for these immortal
but plastic lives

Yes,
we live longer
and can retire
to the computers in our mind
but we forgot the sound
of wind in trees
we forgot that there were stars in the sky

Looking out at Earth that day
I realized something strange
Bob
the first A.I
was more human
than all of us

It is we
who are the machines

The Gift of Art

I've never seen
the light
of an ugly day

When I'm with you
all the pain
just fades away

You've got this
reaction
and it's
turning me
on

You
fill
my Life
with the
gift
of Art

It lets me know
who we are

We're just
partying
under the stars

You let me know
who you are
and that's all
I could ever
want

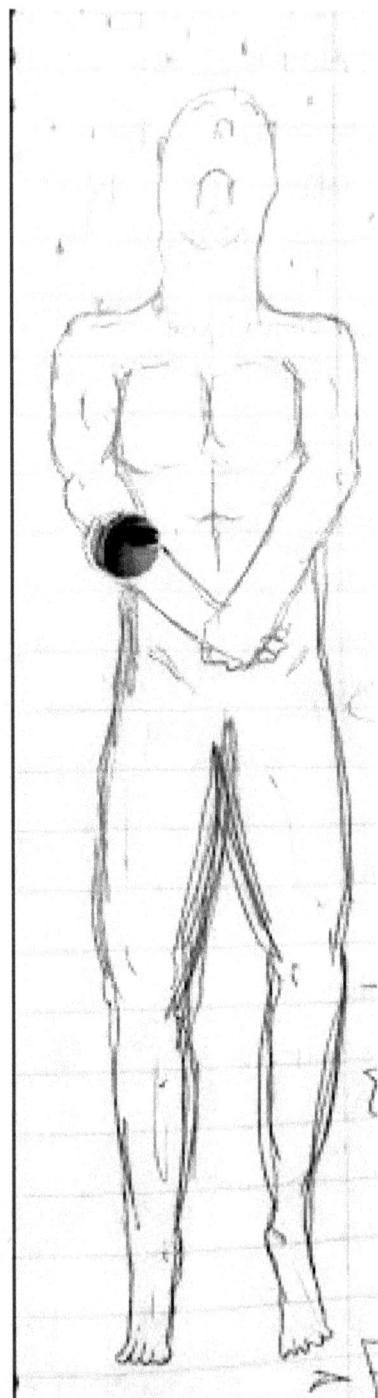

Poetry is Dead

Poetry ain't dead
but if it is
you killed it
cuz when the new shit
came out, man
you just couldn't
get with it

You were too busy waiting
for the old white dude
in the faded sweater
but if ya let me
then I'll show ya something
better

Like

Poetry
can be found
in a child's first
words

Poetry
can be found

in the song
of a bird

Poetry
can be
grammatically
incorrect

Poetry
can sound like a bullet hole
to the neck

Poetry is always done
and never done just yet
and if someone
tells you they're a poet
tell em'
good luck kid

Because didn't you hear?

Poetry is dead

Back to Sleep

I wake up
and there's nothing
on the news
but blood

So I go back
to sleep
and dream
of my love

Then I dream
that a gun is pressed
to the back of my head
and it feels like the sun
shining down on a
flower bed

Then sometimes I wake up
and there's nothing
but pillars of dust
and the slow
steady stroke
of the artist's brush

So I go back
to sleep
and dream
of my love

If I could stay there in that place
I would

I would

Death Touched Me

Death touched me
and now I can't write
anything that's true

I'll lie to you
and tell you a story
where everyone lives

But I'll drown them
when I'm through

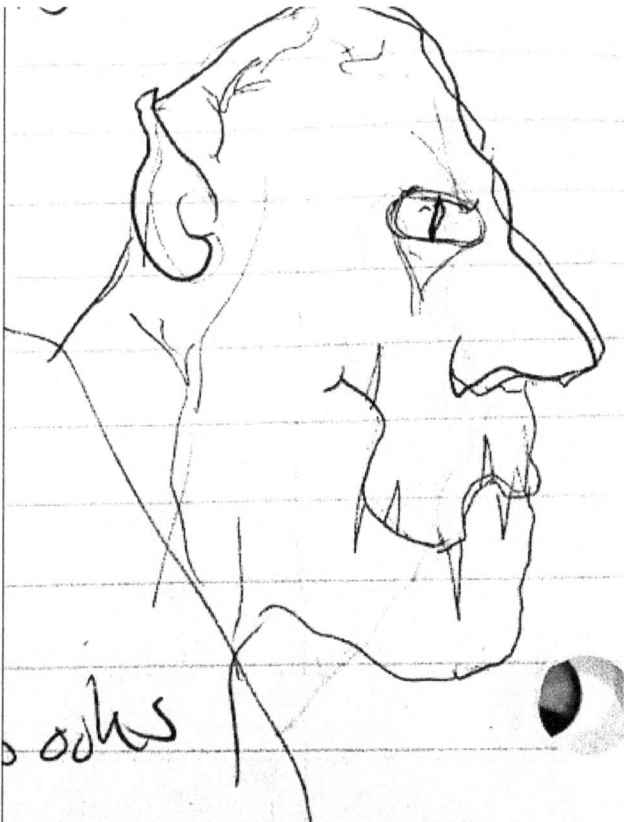

How's it Feel?

How's it feel
when you're feeling sick
and all the Doctor wants to talk about
is the mother fucking bill?

How's it feel
when you're feeling cold?

When the heats cut off
you start wearing extra clothes

How's it feel
when you're feeling sad?

Yeah, they shot your only son
and they shot him in the back

How's it feel
when you're feeling hurt?

It doesn't matter how you feel
man just
Work!
Work!
Work!

How's it feel
when you're feeling old?

You're fucking twenty four
you got a broken soul

Because you feel
what these others
only talk about in theory

They try to spit these numbers
but they'll never illustrate me

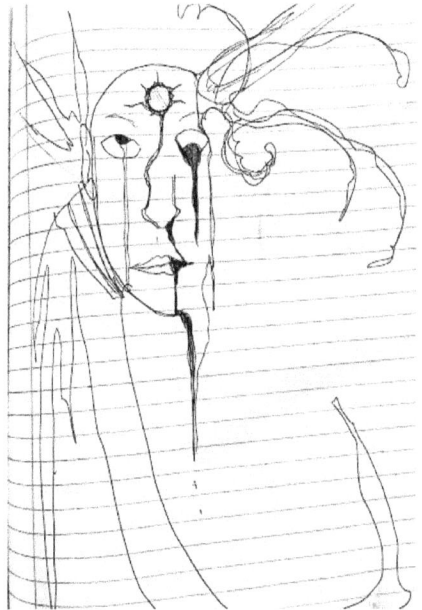

I swear this shit
drives me fucking crazy

One day robots in the sky
will try to replace me

Hah!

With a mother fucking jerk
but the one thing you can't replace
is this single fucking word

Love

Slow

It feels so nice
to walk without a purpose
to walk so slow
people start throwing out curses

"Hey man, get the fuck out of my way,
I got places to go!"

"Well I don't, so
sorry bud. I'm walking slow."

I'm walking so slow
it's like I'm not even moving
like the flower
that reaches for the sun
when no one is looking

I watch a single leaf
fall from a tree

The light shines through
its veins
and tells me I'm free

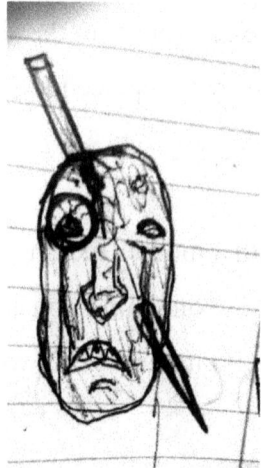

Only Me

Sitting by the lake
reading dispatches
from the war

The leaves skim
the chocolate pool
and take flight off the moor

What are we fighting for!?

A crooked dead tree shivers
all over
beneath its bony fingers
a memorial statue to a donor

Who was Fern L. Adams
and what did she hope for?

An oily green beetle
runs across my feet
the wind carries him
into the grass
and a bird sings for me

Only me

Support the Troops

Could anything kill the beauty
of this college campus
more than soldiers marching in cammo?

They litter the ground
like trash from a riot

They are salesmen of death
but I'm not buying

They shout out their orders
as if their important

They savor the ugliest words
like *ammo*
and *mortar*

They're so damn young
and I feel so old

Time for me to go home
and hold my love

Tight

Our Song

You sing a cruel
melody
bones at your feet
but that's our song

And it floats up to
me
like a red balloon

You got a scar
running down your cheek
eyes that never bleed
because they're stone

But they still capture me
and pull me close
into your arms

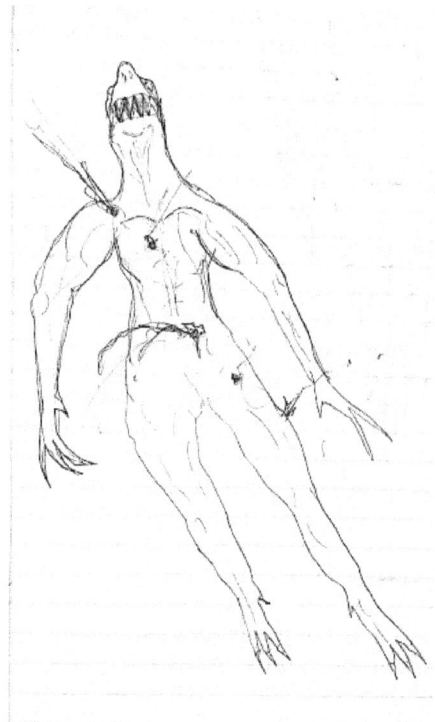

Spring

Time for the beautiful girls
to sprout out of the ground
like poisonous mushrooms

And the copperheads
to snap at the boy's ankles

Time for the old man
to settle back into his job
of sighing and crying

I never knew why he sighed
but now I know why

Now I know why

Crayons

The children of Syria
only reach
for the red crayon

Tiny ears
strain to hear
the day's song

Tiny hands
I could hold
like a shell

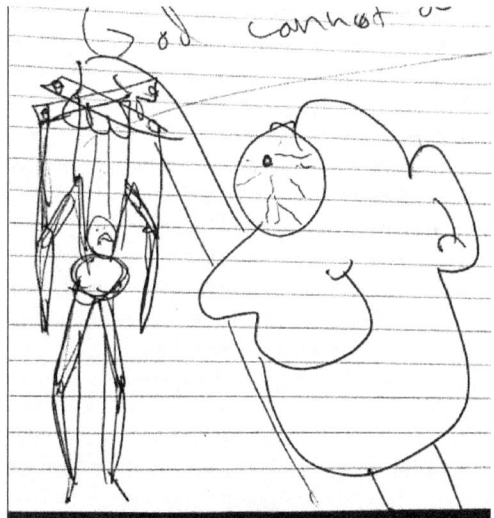

Tiny tears
emptied
from this well

Give my mind
something else
to prey on

Hide the
crayons

Reluctant Lovers

The preschool yard
was overrun
by crows
this morning

They belched
and barked
from behind the fog
in all their
dark glory

I met a big
white dog
named Andy
on my way
to get coffee

I laid my head
on his back
like a carpet

He's a bear
who would
never harm me

I hear the crunch
of the leaf's corpse

I see the mossy copper
cannon
sleeping
in the dream forest

Is there anything
more perfect
than this beautiful girl
in this beat up car
with just enough time
to ignore us?

The cold
and I,
reluctant lovers

Gram

This coke tastes like
Clorox
we all agree

A Greek chorus
humming along to this
tragedy

We could tear
this dealer
limb from limb
with Dionysian glee

But the golden rule
prevails

Do enough of anything
and you'll start to feel
the nails

So we feel our heads
turn into swimming pools
chlorine in our eyes and nose

No mother there
to wipe away

our fuzzy frowns
with a towel
soaked in love

So I slide
onto your shoulder
feeling the fire in my face
grow

I wouldn't even call this coke

Just one more gram to go

Nothing Will Ever Be the Same

You got a garden snake
wrapped around your finger
like a ring

He's biting at your pinky
but he's got no fangs

The pine cones and gumballs
start coming down
like rain

Seven years from now
my cosmic friend will say

Nothing will ever
be the same

The Beach

We hunted clay
down at the beach

We ran barefoot
across the burning street

We bought butane lighters
to smoke our weed

We swam in the middle
of a hurricane

We laid down on the sand
like it was our grave

We kissed with the wind
to our backs
your hair in your face

Hiding the tears
I can't replace

The Way

Sapphire leaves
parachute
to the ground

The Daoist
by the lake
contemplates
the sound

I go to take his
picture
with my phone
made by slaves

Upon the
flash
his frown
meets my gaze

And his eyes
say

I haven't found
the Way